Nia & Khalid

A book for sister.
A book for brother.
A book for father.
A book for mother.

"Make family time, reading time!"

Neter Ankh Hotep-El

Dedicated to Asad Frierson and especially
Kira Frierson who was the inspiration behind the title of this volume.
Dry your eyes baby girl.
Peace & Love.

Published by Nah El Publications
1255 Race Track Road
Sumter, S.C. 29153
Cover design by Neterankhhotep-El for Soul Rhymer Productions
All rights reserved. No part of this publication may be reproduced, stored in a retrieval system,
or transmitted in any form or by any means, electronic, mechanical, including photocopying,
recording, or otherwise, without the written permission of the publisher.
Copyright © 2016 Nia & Khalid Bye Bye Cry Baby by Neterankhhotep-El

Coming Soon!!!

Nia & Khalid

Book 3

Hair & Skin

Hello. Peace. Hi!
My name is Khalid.
I'm 7 years old.

I have a little sister.
She's 5 years old.
She's about to be 6.
She's a BIG CRY BABY!

She cries over
EVERYTHING!!!

EVERYTHING!!!

EVERYTHING!!!

EVERYTHING!!!

Nia is crying because she lost her favorite book.

Book

Book

Book

I Can't Find My Book!!!

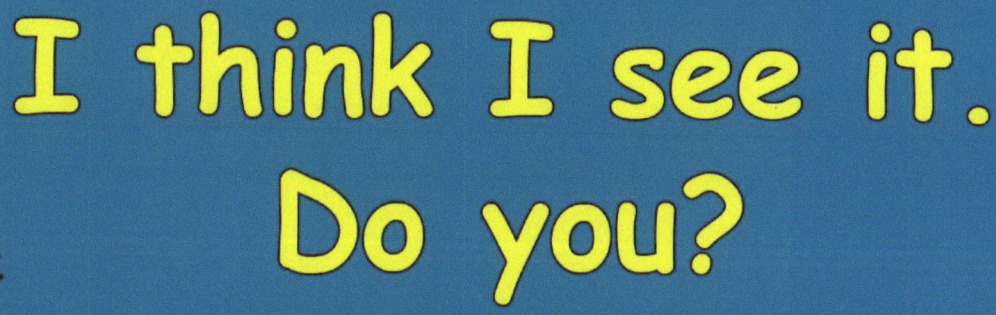

I think I see it.
Do you?

Do you?

Do you?

Do you?

Nia was playing with her toys and broke one.

We had asparagus for dinner but my little sister doesn't like asparagus.

I ate ALL my asparagus!
Asparagus is my favorite vegetable!

asparagus

asparagus

asparagus

asparagus

Nia... It's almost time for bed. Mommy said to take a bath first.

bath
bath
bath
bath

KNOCK!!
KNOCK!!

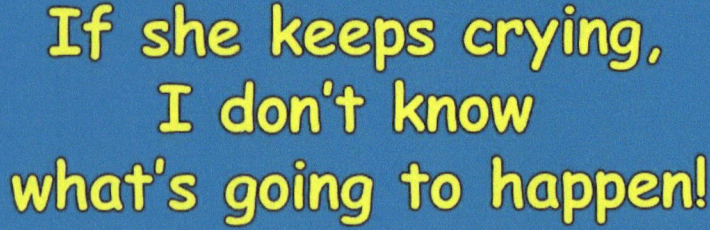

If she keeps crying,
I don't know
what's going to happen!

crying

crying

crying

crying

Nia, you better stop crying before...

That was my little sister Nia floating away.
Bye Bye Cry Baby!!!

The End.

The End.   The End.

Other Books Also Available From The Author

1. Unspoken Words, Beautifully Written

2. Nia & Khalid What Rhymes With...???

3. Black Women Crying Out For Love And Help

4. A Chaotic Love

5. Boys Don't Keep Diaries (Malik's Journal)